Racial Stories

Tales of Three Cities

Eleanor Curry

iUniverse, Inc.
New York   Bloomington

Racial Stories
Tales of Three Cities

iUniverse books may be ordered through booksellers or by contacting:

iUniverse
1663 Liberty Drive
Bloomington, IN 47403
www.iuniverse.com
1-800-Authors (1-800-288-4677)

Because of the dynamic nature of the Internet, any Web addresses or links contained in this book may have changed since publication and may no longer be valid.

ISBN: 978-1-4401-3912-3 (sc)
ISBN: 978-1-4401-3914-7 (dj)
ISBN: 978-1-4401-3913-0 (ebk)

Printed in the United States of America

iUniverse rev. date: 6/23/2009

CONTENTS

Acknowledgments

Brenda Davis, my oldest daughter, convinced me to write these stories, detailing how her Dad and I raised eight children in the United States of America, in spite of the reported tensions, particularly between Black people and White people in our country.

Joseph Bailey, a mentor from the United Crusade (now the United Way), who guided me in the 1950's on "Ten Secrets of Solid Leadership."

Tia Creighton, Consultant Representative of the Peninsula Library System, San Mateo, California. A month long series of events centered on The Big Read, an initiative of the National Endowment of the Arts, in partnership with the Institute of Museum and Library Services and Arts Midwest, focusing on the reading of To Kill a Mockingbird (2007).

Claire Mack, a Civic leader, one of the first local people declaring a need to change the educational system by noting "separated public schools being unequal." She worked on Staff as a Community Specialist from 1969-1979 to enhance the lives of low income children. Claire became the first African American Mayor in the City of San Mateo.

Ruth Nagler, Public Library System, Public Relations Consultant, San Mateo County, an advocate of promoting racial harmony from the early 1960's through the 1980's, and promoting Desegregation in the San Mateo City Schools as a Board Member.

Erma Jean Prothro, Psychologist, advocate of Family & Children's Emotional, Psychological and Spiritual growth, from1974-1978, the Human Relations Director of the San Mateo Elementary School District.

Rona Renner, RN, talk show hostess of CHILDHOOD MATTERS on Radio Station 98.1 F.M., one of the Moderators of a panel discussion entitled "Family Values & Racial Issues," at the Big Read Event that covered To Kill a Mockingbird in April, 2007.

Dorie Vallon Wheeler, a journalism teacher at the Middle School level, who became a "Special

Assignment Instructor," teaching other teachers about the importance of Black History and inclusive behavior toward all students, regardless of color.

Dr. Marguerite A. Wright, Senior Psychologist, Children's Hospital, Oakland California, also a Moderator of the panel discussion entitled "Family Values & Racial Issues," at the Big Read Event that covered To Kill a Mockingbird in April, 2007.

An extra "thanks" to all the parents, teachers, agencies and organizations that made it possible for every child, regardless of their ethnic identities, to grow in healthy caring neighborhoods.

San Carlos, California   Eleanor Williams-Curry
April 2009

PREFACE

I have experienced real life racial issues personally and in the public domain from the time I was four years old to the present day. I have witnessed other African American adults left bitter by the pains caused by the blunt intrusion of racism. I have seen far too many children struggling over their very first encounter with prejudice and discrimination.

I have witnessed positive changes, where people from different racial groups learned about each other making choices to be good neighbors instead of unknown hostile enemies. I realize it is difficult for some of our parents to concentrate on events in

the public domain, when far too many of our homes are falling apart, because of severe economic conditions.

Due to a lack of "the powerful training one receives when moving from the classroom, to the boardroom, from the schoolhouse to the statehouse, from college to congress…" appears to be standard expectations for the bulk of most middle-class Americans. ("Dimensions of Learning," University of Baltimore.)

I entered the American scene without such a fundamental powerbase. I came from a background of segregated laws, invisible attention, and serious overt restrictions.

My thoughts and reflections will reflect this journey: From the high school classroom to the first part-time job at 14 years old; from the schoolhouse on the segregated side of town; from the early death of my parents; from an early marriage (for which I was totally unprepared); from community college independent studies programs toward the local church; from emotional desperation to any job available, I moved to higher heights. Housing patterns subjected us to live life in the rawhide of society. Moving from the ghetto of St. Louis, Missouri, to integrating an all white neighborhood in the same city, was a sharp reality of opposites. Next a move to the projects of San Francisco made one wonder "where is God?" Finally, the suburbs of San Mateo County, California, pinpointed another phase of life that is America.

Here are the challenges, choices, and compromises. Here are the failures, frustrations, and freedoms. Here are successful attitudes, beautiful friendships, and creative peace of one's personal journey inside the racial atmospheric pressure fields.

PART ONE: SAINT LOUIS, MISSOURI

All manners, feelings, or positions, with regard to a person, can be changed whether with positive or negative behaviors. Have we ever considered how the weather plays a big role in our attitudes? We know it rains on the just, the unjust. We know the sun shines. We know of the floods. We know of the seasons. We know of the earthquakes. Are we prepared when the weather brings its various seasons? Is it too late for some critical thinking from large bodies of people to prepare ourselves with plans to change the racially insulting practices that divide our country?

1 THAT'S NOT FAIR, 1936

"Boys and girls," the teacher said, as she rang a small bell for order, "I have a treat for one person who finishes their essay first. That person will take today's message to the teachers on the second floor." Eleanor, with steady big brown eyes, a perfect match for her cinnamon colored skin, was too excited. She believed she was the fastest one to finish anything having to do with writing. She quickly completed her paper. She rushed from her desk, which was at the front of the classroom, placed her paper on the teacher's desk, waiting to hear that she had finished first. She patiently stood there.

"Eleanor, take your paper back to your seat. Review it before you give it to me." She looked very stern. "No one could finish that fast and not have an error." Eleanor reluctantly did as she was ordered.

Moments later, another student walks up to the teacher's desk. "Miss Johnson, I doubled checked my paper," Minnie Walton said too sweetly. Standing there with her high yellow skin and head full of Shirley Temple's curls, she threw her head back so her curls would shake. "I think this might be the way you want it to look. Could you check it please?"

"Minnie, you have exactly what I want." Miss Johnson was smiling. "Boys and girls, let's give Minnie a hand for doing a good job. She wins, ready to deliver the message."

"That's not fair!" Eleanor shouts from her seat. She was shocked. "That's not fair! I was first!" Eleanor rubbed her short black braided hair and looked down at her dark colored hands. You picked her because you think she's cute."

"Stop it right now!" Miss Johnson was looking stern again. "If you utter another word, Eleanor, you'll be suspended for the rest of the week." Eleanor sat shaken and sullen until 3:00 p.m. when school was dismissed.

Once home, her story poured out faster than running water. "Oh Momma, I hate being dark. I hate these thick ugly braids. Why can't my skin be light and why can't I have curly hair?" Tears are flowing as she repeats the happenings of the morning. "That's not fair." Eleanor wipes her hand across her face.

"Well, baby," Mom is very calm, yet firm, "whatever made you think life is fair? Stop whining about changing your God given looks. God made you the way He wanted you. He gave you a brain so you would be smarter than most people. So use your brain. Do not ever deny the beauty God wanted you to be. Curly hair does not give you extra sense. When you go to school tomorrow, tell Miss Johnson you're sorry for screaming out in class."

"But, Momma, she was the one who was wrong. Do I have to do that in front of the class?" Eleanor is startled at her mother's order.

"The sooner you straighten this out, the better you'll feel." Momma hugged me close. "Do your part, watch life get fair."

2 THE DEAF MUTE COLONY, 1953

We're living in a rental, a beautiful three bedroom house sold out from under us. We had to be out within 30 days. I went to see Big Charlie, the light complexion, cigar smoking Real Estate dealer. He discretely was known for attempting to break down housing segregation. This meant sending two colored volunteers to rent apartments. Often they would receive a bogus negative response from the owners. Big Charlie would follow up by sending two white volunteers to the exact same house, and they would be accepted. Once he heard my dilemma, he began to drum his fingers on his large cedar desk saying, "I think I have the perfect house for you and your little family. There's one problem though.

"What is the problem?" I inquire confused; concerned about the deadline date that was getting shorter and shorter, "The house is in the middle of a white neighborhood actually. Have you ever lived near any white families?

"No, but I have worked for them. They seem just like anyone else. What's the big deal?

"On second thought, you'll do just fine. You can move in immediately. Sign right here on the bottom line. This is a year's lease. Call me anytime."

We moved in the following week. The first neighbor I saw was in a wheelchair trying to get out. I walked over to her asking, "Can I help you?" She focused her eyes swiftly away as if she did not see me. I backed away thinking she couldn't hear me. Can you believe for the next five months none of the people in that entire block ever spoke to our family? Finally, I saw one woman walking to the grocery store. I quickly rushed to her saying, "Hello, I am one of your neighbors..." She glanced at me and swiftly began <u>running</u> to the store.

I became very uncomfortable thrown off guard. My husband came home from work that evening, sensing something was wrong. "Are you O. K.?" I spoke very low, "There's something wrong with this neighborhood. The people cannot see or hear me when I move towards to them. I think we are living in a deaf mute colony."

"Oh my goodness, you're describing prejudice, honey." He pauses. I'm dumbfounded shouting, "That's what prejudice feels like!" I realized I had to protect our five children. The next morning I told them cheerfully, "I'm going to set up a tea party area right on the back porch. We'll have a great time when you come home from school. Only one rule: Don't leave the back porch. Within a few weeks all the children their age were coming to the back porch to play. When one mother who lived at the end of the block came to pick up her six year old daughter, Patty, the daughter was screaming, "I don't want to go home. It's no fun. I want to stay and play with the colored' kids." Her mother held her tighter, dragging her home. Just a few days later, her mother was knocking at my door. Upon opening the door, she quickly uttered, "Welcome to the neighborhood."

Well! I was flabbergasted, feeling warmer than the 97degree temperature. Five months later, most of the women were waving, talking and acting like real neighbors, while at the clothesline in the backyard. We had more in common than we ever knew. We still lived under segregated laws, but never discussed the subject.

Lucille and Robert became good friends too. "Lucille", I asked directly, "Why did you guys avoid and not speak to us when we first moved in here last year?" "Oh, Eleanor, Lucille responds, "Robert had read all about the shootings and cuttings in the colored paper. The paper wrote how your people got drunk on Friday and Saturday nights, cutting each other, ending up either in the hospital or in jail." Rushing on, she said, "Finally, we began to realize that that's not the way you were at all. In fact, your family was very quiet. We felt bad misjudging you." She grabbed my free hand, and we walked the entire backyard, waving at the other neighbors.

Before the Fourth of July rolled around, Patty ran to the back porch, shouting, "Mrs. Curry, I asked Mommy if we could invite you all to the picnic and she said 'YES'."

3 SEWING CLASS DEBACLE, 1953

Although I felt better with the neighbors, loneliness would creep up early evenings. The daily newspaper carried a picture of a dress pattern. Yearnings returned to memories of long winter months when Mother taught us to make crafts. I recalled being the first teenage girl to study Industrial Arts at local Sumner High School. I copied the newspaper pattern. I went to the fabric store, bought three yards of pale yellow cotton pique, cost - 55 cents a yard. I'm ready. After making a paper pattern, placing it on the pretty material, plus cutting out a white V-neck yoke, I was ready to sew. It took me nearly two weeks to hand-stitch my new dress. My husband was surprised when I modeled this new creation for him.

We went to his Mom's house for dinner on a warm summer Friday evening.

"Where did you get that cute dress?" she noticed the dress.

"I made it," I uttered shyly.

"Do you have a sewing machine?" She inquired intently.

"No. I stitched it by hand," I said proudly.

"Earl," she looked toward her son, "Honey you need to buy your wife a sewing machine."

The next payday, which happened on the first and fifteenth of the month, Earl bought me a new sewing machine. A coupon was enclosed offering an eight-week sewing class, teaching beginners how to sew. I enrolled in the class. Little did I realize how living under segregated laws would affect the sewing class.

Mrs. Walker, a white home economics teacher, had a friendly smile, sparkling blue eyes, and possibly a size 14, welcomed the 16 enrollees with genuine stability. She encouraged all of us to seek help as necessary. The enrollment consisted of a dozen white women and five colored women, ranging in age from their mid-twenties to early thirties. When we were first given our seats, it didn't occur to me that we were separated by a long sliding door. I simply thought the other students were working at an advanced level. Four weeks later, Mrs. Walker became ill.

"Eleanor," she said, struggling with severe coughing, "you are the most advanced student in the class. Your dress is near completion." She pulled a handkerchief to her mouth. "I'd like to ask a favor. Can you come an hour earlier and teach the class until I feel better?"

"Of course!" I exclaimed without hesitation. "What will I have to do?"

"Take the roll call. Review each student's progress. Don't let anyone move ahead if they have not followed the instruction guide-sheet." Her voice drops to a whisper.

""That's all?" I asked, feeling pleased I'm being chosen.

"Yes." She says slowly. "I hope to return in two weeks. Thanks Eleanor."

The following Tuesday evening, I encounter the long sliding door. The white students were on one side, coloreds on the other side. The entire class was for beginners.

"Good evening, everybody." I waited until all were seated. "Mrs. Walker will not be here for a couple of weeks. She put me in charge. I'd like to leave this door open, so we can get our work done faster. We can help each other easier, too. Is that clear? Any questions?" I asked courageously. Total silence. This time I was ready for the quietness sweeping over the room. I silently counted to five seconds.

"Since there aren't any questions, let's get started. We'll work in groups of three. Introduce yourselves; I'll visit each team throughout our time together. We can complete our garments while Mrs. White is recuperating. She'll be thrilled at discovering how smart you are. Lets' get started." Everybody worked in harmony without any complaints. Mrs. Walker was out longer than she had planned, returning for the last two sessions.

The class was enthusiastic and anxious to greet Mrs. Walker. All the garments were finished. Our teacher was thrilled for a moment. She did the strangest thing. She placed her hands on her hips, took a deep breath and hissed at us, "Move back to your correct seats." She reached over and furiously pulled the long sliding door to its former position. The class was segregated again. She stood stiffly by the half opened door. "I have something for you." She said as normal as possible to the white students. It was a large envelop with their names on the outside. She turned to us saying, "I hope you enjoyed learning how to sew. Class is dismissed." She was not acting like the Mrs. Walker we knew.

"Mrs. Walker," I asked, jumping from my seat. "What's going on? I opened that door on purpose. We worked well together. We thought you would be pleased. What's wrong?

"Eleanor, remain after class. I have something to tell you." She looked full of pain. Is she sick again?

The white students grabbed their belongings, mouthed a pitiful "good-bye" and rushed from the class. Three of the colored students hesitated, held their eyes down, mumbling good-byes. One languished behind, staring at me, placing her finger over her lips, as if to warn me: "Don't say anything else."

"What was that all about?" I'm getting angry! "Why didn't we get any large envelopes? We finished our outfits too. What happen to you?" Suddenly I stop, as I focused on Mrs. Walker's eyes. She's quietly crying, the blood was drained from her face.

"Oh! Eleanor. I'm so sick of what people call the law!" She continues with a belligerent, angry tone. "I hate to tell you the things that happened since I left you in charge of the class. I knew you were my best student. Someone complained to the Manager that you had changed the arrangement in the room. He called me. I explained to him why I chose you.

"Don't be putting uppity ideas in that colored gal's head, making her think she's smarter than our precious white women. You know the law. You better straighten this out before your reputation gets ruined. You don't want people to think you're a niggerlover," she imitated his crude voice as he spoke to Mrs. Walker in a very menacing manner. "He made me feel so unclean. I hate these stupid rules." Mrs. Walker was oblivious to my presence. "Everything has to stay segregated. Even when they know segregation does not work. This is disgusting!" She turns back to me. "The certificates were all job offerings from the large companies. None of the companies will hire colored people to work for their white clients." She laughs in an ironic fashion.

"My best student is colored and I can't offer her a job. I can offer you a job at my house. You can make my five year old daughter some petticoats and a few dresses. Oh! Eleanor, I'm so embarrassed." Speechless, I stare at her in total disbelief.

"Say something." She moved toward me reaching for my hand. "Say anything." I backed away from her gesture. How could I internalize the last ten minutes? I felt suffocated.

"Good-bye, Mrs. Walker." I sound civil. Yet, I'm drained, disgusted and dismayed. I can't swallow that gut level anger. I can't see her anymore. Still courteous, I firmly say, "Call me when you are better Mrs. Walker." I back out of the classroom, slamming the door.

"Damn!" I am talking to myself as I wait for the segregated bus to take me to my side of town. I don't even cuss. For some reason, damn seems to fit. What am I going to do now? I thought I was going to have a job. Eight weeks completed and no job.

Mrs. Walker called a few weeks later. Her husband had a stroke. She had to go to work full time. I began making clothes for her little girl. Next thing I knew, I had placed a sign in our window making clothes for other little girls, sizes 6X to size 12 for preteens. Mrs. Walker and I became telephone friends, being careful never to meet in any public places. We stayed acquainted in spite of the segregated laws.

4 MANY JOBS, LITTLE MONEY, 1947-1953

Earl's steady job was parking cars in a downtown shopping complex. He was on duty from 8 A.M. to 4:30 P.M., five days a week. He cleaned professional offices from 6:00 P.M to 8:30 P.M., at a minimum of two days each week. Plus, on too many Saturdays to count, he was a handyman. He painted houses either inside or outside. He helped people move, hauling their furniture without any benefit of insurance. He was constantly trying to earn enough money to take care of our family. He labeled all this extra work "odd jobs."

When I decided I should find a job to help with the income, he refused to hear me. "Children need their mother at home." He was unshaken about this requirement. "Too many kids go astray because the parents are not there. That's it. OK?"

I planned odd jobs for myself that would keep me at home with our children. My tasks became baby-sitting, sewing clothes for adults, and braiding little girls' hair. I earned hugs, small change, and heart-felt "thank you so much." We had too much month, but not enough money.

Meanwhile, strife was developing at Earl's Union Street Garage facility. Although the colored workers were in the Union, most of them worked the normal eight- hour a day shift. Management wanted the colored men to work overtime without getting double pay. Most of the colored guys were stressed out thinking they had no choice. They decided to agree in order to keep their jobs. One of them approached Earl to join their ranks, too, without the double pay.

"No! We get double pay or they find somebody else," Earl stated in a steady determined voice. "The white guys get double pay. We should get double pay, too."

The colored guys spread the word that Earl was a troublemaker. Earl tried to convince them to stand firm. They capitulated, instead. Yet Earl refused to accept this unfair plan. The main two bosses over the colored team were split because of Earl's stance. One perceived Earl as a strong-principled man, while the other considered Earl "too big for his britches and I want him out of here."

When Earl came home, he said nothing to me about all this turmoil. "I've had enough of working so hard and getting such little pay." He sounded weary, but undefeated. "I think I have a better solution."

Whenever Earl was talking out loud, deep in concentration, I had learned to patiently wait for the next comment. I was dumbfounded, wondering what could we do, or where could we go, I stood still.

"Eleanor, I'm tired of working just to pay rent and feed us." Earl perks up speaking swiftly. "Let's move to California. What do you think?

"If you think we should, I'll do whatever you want to do," I whispered (while internally – I wondered silently is he crazy?). I only knew California as one of the 48 states.

"Good!" He smiled broadly. "That means YES!" "When are we going?" I asked, touching my throat. "I'm leaving next week." He was pumped up and extra pleased. "I'll send for you and the kids in a couple of months."

Earl purchased a powder blue station wagon with his few savings. One of his sisters paid the rest. He filled up the gas tank, gave me a big bear hug and a kiss. He started driving to California five days after our conversation.

Suddenly, I encountered two unrelated challenges: Once Earl had left I had to dispose of the household furnishings. The gossiping neighbors came, not to support his actions, but to pry into our affairs. Several of us were hanging clothes in the long back yard.

"Where did your husband go, Mrs. Curry?" one neighbor asked pointedly, smirking.

"He went to California. He'll send for us later," I replied without hesitation.

"Oh, you poor thing. Don't you know you ain't never going' to see that man again?" She was proud of her worthless knowledge. "Honey, colored men ain't what you think. Once they get gone, they are gone for good."

I snatched up my clothes basket, rushing back to my apartment. I slammed my door shut, hearing the loud laughter coming from the other women. I felt sadder and sadder for the next few months. We could no longer pay any rent. Rosa, one of Earl's older sisters, moved our five children and me into her five bed room home. She treated us like royalty. Six weeks later, we were able to move from her home, taking a train to California.

Earl lived with his oldest sister, Adele, in San Mateo, California. He became a carpenter and joined the Union. The first monies he was able to save, he bought train tickets for one adult and three children. Not enough tickets for the other two. I quickly made a call, "What happened to the other train tickets for the two younger kids?" Earl laughs, "When I was looking for a house, I couldn't find anything for seven people. I dropped the number to 3 kids. I forgot we had 5 kids. Get ready. I love you." We moved to the Crocker Amazon Housing Project, in San Francisco, California, in 1955.

PART TWO: SAN FRANCISCO, CALIFORNIA

San Francisco, the City that knows how, the City of hills, Cable cars and inspiring creative people. Imagine, facing no more Jim Crow laws, no discrimination and plenty of sunshiny days. The last major earthquake was in 1906. Have we finally arrived to the land of milk and honey?

5 WELCOME TO SAN FRANCISCO, 1955

We are being driven from the train station to our new home by Aunt Adell, Earl's oldest sister.

"Honey, my brother was so anxious to get you and the kids here, the house I'm taking you to, was all he could find." Aunt Adele uttered these words very casual and pleasant.

"We're so happy to be here, I'm sure both of you did your best." I couldn't believe I would finally see my husband after all these months.

Hugh trees lined both sides of the street. I was impressed with the hills, the clear blue sky, and such a bright sunny afternoon.

Quickly she turned the car off the main thoroughfare on to a dirt bumpy road. The dirt road stretched straight ahead curving into a cluster of one story shack houses sitting on top of stilts, a foot and a half tall. I glanced out the right side car window. Several little children were playing in the dirt under a few of these houses. I was taken aback, silently thinking that this could not be the City that I had heard so much about. "Who lives in a place like this?" I barely whispered. The houses were the same size, the same color, and had the same look of desolation.

"You will in a minute." Aunt Adele pulled right in front of the next "shack," opened her side of the door, walked up three wooden steps, and put a key into the lock. "Here's your new house," she said, looking directly at my shocked face. "It'll get better. Are you okay?

"Of course," I lied. "Just a little surprised at the houses being on stilts." The interior was spanking clean, consisting of a kitchen, two large bedrooms, a bathroom and no living room. Adele handed me the door key.

"Earl should be off work in a couple more hours." Adele leans over, pecks me on the cheek, attempting to be cheerful. "Welcome to San Francisco."

6 INTEGRATE, 1ST GRADE

The six-year old son came home from his new school, anxious to tell his mother the new word he had learned at school. The word was "integrate."

"The teacher told us how to integrate today, Mama." The mother waited. "Can I have a cookie?" he asked in the next breath. End of comment.

Two days later he ran through the front door straight to the kitchen where his mother was preparing his lunch.

"Guess what, Mama? I know how to integrate now," he said proudly.

"What do you mean?" The mother stopped cooking, thinking this is important to him. It's time to listen.

"Today at recess, I played with the white kids, the Oriental kids, the Mexican kids, and I even played with some of those colored kids." He was elated and smiling.

"Hold on." The mother said moving closer, reaching for his hand. "When we lived in Missouri we were called Negroes. Sometimes we were called 'coloreds.'

"Wait a minute." He backed away from his mother, immediately stopped smiling.

"You're a Negro? Is Daddy a Negro? All of us in this house are Negroes? Me, too?"

"That's right," the mother replied, attempting to reassure him that everything was O.K. She pulled him closer, hugging him. "No! No! No!" He started crying. The mother rubbed his upper back, really concerned at his reactions. "What's the matter, honey? Why are you crying? "We can't be colored!" He was bewildered, shaking his head back and forth.

"They throw erasers at each other and have to sit in the naughty corner a lot!"

"Some of them might act up. Everybody acts up sometimes." The mother explained as best she could.

He sat very quiet. The mother waited, rubbing one of his hands, realizing the next few minutes would be critical for him.

"What did you think you were before now?" the mother asked calmly.

"I thought I was English, because that's how we talk."

7 White Pastor, Colored Family

Hunter's Point, San Francisco, 1961. Our last child was 8 months old. We had lived at 56 West Point Road in Hunter's Point for less than a year, when a white man with a minister's collar knocked at our door that summertime afternoon. I glanced through our keyhole, noticed his attire and immediately thought that he must be lost. I opened the door.

"Hello. My name is Pastor John Ratcliff." "If you don't have a church home, would you like to join our missionary church?

"We haven't been in the area long enough to know where the churches are." I was still a little surprised. "Where is your church located?

"It's very close." He was very polite while reaching for a card and other literature to give me.

"We have all the traditional things, Sunday School classes at 9:30 AM, regular church services at 11:00 AM, and always Orientation for new members. I hope you'll become one of our new members.

"I'll have to talk to my husband when he comes home from work." I'm still in awe from his request. "We are the Curry family if you need our name.

"Oh! Yes! I forgot to ask you your name. I also neglected to tell you we belong to the Lutheran faith. I'm Pastor of the Bayview Lutheran Church. Thanks for your time. I'll be waiting to hear from you. Good bye, Mrs. Curry."

Many questions paraded cross my thoughts. What is a Lutheran? Do white people really go to church? Why was he knocking on our door instead of working with the whites?

Once my husband came home from work and heard of our visitor, we discussed the need for our children to receive some Christian training. We decided to join that specific church. We did not know of any other churches. It was great when we first attended to discover several other colored families. We attended Orientation Classes. I was surprised to learn how the Lutherans taught us a different message. We heard over and over again, during the eight weeks classes about how GOD loves those who want to be saved. GOD represents love, not hate. GOD gave his only begotten Son, Jesus Christ, so whosoever believed in him would have everlasting life. We heard very little to nothing regarding "if you don't behave, you could burn in Hell, or the Devil will get you, if you don't watch out."

This version of GOD was so strong. I definitely wanted my family to find this GOD the Lutherans taught about being a GOD of love. We had our entire family baptized at the Bayview Lutheran Church on Mother's Day, 1961. Months later Pastor Ratcliff asked me to become President of the Ladies Guild. This gave me an opportunity to select programs with other church leaders. I had an opportunity to represent our church at various events with other Lutheran Churches in the State of California. Two events were very graphic from my involvement.

"Sister Curry, I'd like you to represent our Church at the Missionary Symposium next week." Pastor was full of joy as he explained my duties. "Mainly you will speak before a panel of missionary leaders. Ask them for at least twenty pews for our church.

"Will they just give them to us?" I asked confused. "Why would they give them away? Do we have to pay anything down on these pews?

"No, Sister Curry," Pastor was smiling, "We are a missionary church. The richer congregations help support the smaller ones. Once you arrive at the hotel, they will give you an application to fill out with our request for the pews. There'll be probably a dozen or two other smaller congregations seeking assistance, too. Normally no more than five requests are chosen a year. So, remember, Sister Curry, make a good solid case and try to get the pews."

My husband and I arrived at the hotel in Monterey on Friday evening. Early Saturday morning, breakfast time, everyone was busy walking around preparing for the day's events. I noticed the large sign over one door "Missionary Applications." I hasten to that area, pleased that I'd found it. Once entering the room, at least a dozen people were already in line waiting for their papers. I finished my application. A sign to wear around my neck was # 9 in bold black on a white background.

An elder women was saying, "When you hear your number called, you'll speak before the panel of judges and make your request." I sat in the designated area awaiting my turn. The requests were unbelievable. They asked for start-up items, including money. They would say:

"We need funds to start building our church. Right now we're using a trailer." "We are paying rent at a church near our houses. It's beginning to cost too much."

"We don't have any Bibles and cannot afford to buy any right now."

"I'd like to request a desk and chair for our minister so he won't have to carry his sermons back and forth each week."

I sat amazed hearing their stories. Finally my turn came. I felt very confident. "Good Morning Honorable Judges," glancing from one to the other. "I'm here today representing Bayview Lutheran Church in San Francisco." I pause. "After hearing our other fellow Christians, I find their needs far greater than ours. I relinquish our request. Please withdraw our slot for those who seem more in need. Thank you for your time." I quickly turned and walked from the room. The minute I was outside, I heard Pastor Ratcliff's voice, "make a good case for the pews." "OH NO!" I cried out to no one in particular, what made me say such a stupid thing? How will I ever explain to Pastor Radcliff those words coming from my mouth? Why did I give away our chance? I walked around the hotel premises' three times, attempting to quiet the chatter from my head. My nerves made me tremble. I dare not tell my husband.

I am perplexed. I'd better get a grip and pretend to act pleasant. Thank goodness it was time for lunch. During lunch, people were chatty and friendly, yet I couldn't say word. I was preoccupied through the rest of the day's workshop and dinner! What did I do? Who can I tell? I actually gave our chance away to have new pews. I finally prayed for God to give me an answer to this dilemma. I dropped off to an unfitting sleep.

The next morning, everybody returns to the Applications Area for the announcement of the five finalists. I enter the room. I decide to report the winners to Pastor, never confessing the blunder I had made. Once seated, the procedure began. The Presiding Judge called for order. A prayer and a reading of scripture were presented. The Judge began to talk.

"We have some unfinished business from yesterday to take of care before we discuss the finalists. Is applicant number 9 present?" I slowly raise my hand.

"Please come to the podium. Explain to the panel your actions yesterday. Why did you leave so quickly?

"After hearing the other requests, I felt the needs of the others were greater than ours," I replied uncomfortably.

"Please tell us now what you were sent to request. Are you aware it was not your duty to make the decision you rendered? We have a panel of judges. Do you understand?

"Yes I do, however, that was not my intent. I came to my conclusion merely listening to the other applicants." I was speaking in a slow defensible manner.

"Tell us now, as you were instructed to do yesterday.

"We are a small missionary church in San Francisco. I was sent here to request a minimum of twenty pews." I stopped talking, held my head up and waited.

"Do you still want to relinquish your Pastor's request?

"After a sleepless night and knowing our Pastor's last directive, I realized I did not have the right to ignore his instructions. But, I feel the same way as I did yesterday. I think some of the others take priority over our needs.

"Any more questions for this young lady?" He asked the other judges. "Have a seat. We are not finished with you yet." They began to write notes, passing them to the Presiding Judge. He opened the four notes. He told me to come back to the podium.

"The judges have made a final decision about your actions yesterday and this morning. Due to the unselfish attitude you have displayed, the Committee has voted to give your church the pews as its first order of business." The room participants broke into spontaneous applause as tears rolled down my face. I softly cried as I thanked the Committee. I was overjoyed. The News was wired to Pastor Ratcliff. When I returned home, Doris, the Pastor's wife, hugged me and saying to me in a joking way, "My goodness, Sister Eleanor, what did you do at that convention? So many people have called us, I'm sick of hearing your name."

8 GRACE, PLACE AND RACE CONFERENCE

The Annual event on Grace, Place and Race Conference is being held in Orange County, California, with an attendance of over 600 members. I'm on the morning panel, discussing Dr. Martin Luther King's Non-violence marches, plus why my family became Lutherans. During the question and answer period, right before the adjournment, an elderly woman stood up holding her Bible rather close saying, "Mrs. Curry, I loved your message, but I would not like my daughter to marry one of them. Please respond to my concern."

"One of them what?" I was trying to internalize her question, the room was death-pan silent.

"You know," she was exasperated, continuing, "one of those Negroes."

"I have been married to one of those Negroes for 25 years and nothing has happen to me yet." The room exploded into laughter and loud applause from all of the white parishioners. The leader adjourned the session. Another member rushed up, hugging me joyfully saying, "Sister Curry, you just save our congregation. My daughter is married to a Negro solider. He returned from the Marines wanting to attend the church. The woman raised some much trouble that the church was split down the middle. Thank you so much."

9 POVERTY STRICKEN TO VOLUNTEERING

Joe Bailey, a United Crusade Staff member, became my mentor, when I had no idea what a mentor does for you. "The Hill" was short for Hunter's Point. Over 300 families lived in the area. Most of the services for the residents were at the top of the hill. We had to ride the bus, taking our children under five years of age to the top of the hill so they had a place to play. This caused a burden for most of our families.

"Why can't we have day care services closer to our houses?" I asked a neighbor, who had lived there much longer.

"They won't let us do it." She answered slowly.

"Let's go and tell them what we want. It's not up to them.

"I don't think they'll pay any attention.

"Where are they and when do they meet?

"They meet once a month at the Bay View Community Center."

The Hunter's Point District Council usually met from 11 a.m. until 2:00 p.m. every 1ˢᵗ Monday. Joe Bailey attended those meetings. He asked me if I was interested in volunteering to work on the Council, because all the present Council members did not live on The Hill. Joe instantly began training me. I had stacks of books to read about the community. He quizzed me on issues such as meeting the press, how to teach other children self-discipline, and helping poor citizens find food and clothing for their families. Within eight weeks, he had crammed two years of college into my brain. Next, he smiled saying, "You're on your own now, but I'm right behind you."

The Civil Rights Movement was in high gear. Several large mothers (in stature and weight) ruled The Hill. I was President of the Bret Hart P.T.A., which made me one of the "mothers." There were very few jobs for the young men living on The Hill. A panel, consisting of five representatives from the San Francisco Mayor's office, set up a public hearing in order to find out what obstacles were hindering the young men from finding any type of work.

The dialogue began.

"If it wasn't for the 'Man', I know I could do something," the first speaker grumbled.

"The Man keeps us from getting the stuff we ought to have. I have to help my Mom and my two little sisters. It's tough out here," replied the second person. "We need some real jobs."

These frustrating discourses went on for nearly an hour. Every single comment covered The Man and how The Man was destroying their lives. Finally, one of the upper middle-class white women from the Mayor's office interrupted by asking:

"Would one of you kindly give me the name and telephone number of this Man, so we can stop his interfering with your request to work?"

She appeared puzzled as the entire room erupted into laughter.

However, once the Public Findings were reported back to the Mayor, several companies like PG&E, Pacific Telephone Company, and the United Crusade found jobs for over 30% of the young people who attended the Public Hearing.

10 POLICE COMMUNITY RELATIONS, 1962

On a sunny Thursday afternoon, we heard screams. The screaming became louder, stronger, and more hysterical, turning into deep moaning breathless sounds.

"Don't open that door." I cautioned my children, who were ready to rush outside to see what had happened. One of the daughters ran to the telephone and called a close neighbor to find out if she knew what was going on.

"It's Bobby," the neighbor said quickly, "You know Marie's and Albert's oldest son. I'm not for sure, but I think somebody shot him (16 years old). They think he stole something and got caught trying to run home. They shot him right before he could reach his folks door step. Albert, his dad, is still at work. We might have to go over there and help Marie 'til he comes home. I have to hang up now.

"Somebody shot Bobby, Mama." My daughter's voice was listless. "That's all I could find out."

The sun had gone down. Several of the women on our short street were at Albert's house when he came home from work. Marie was trying to hold back her sobs, now and again saying "Lord have mercy, why my child?" "Lord have mercy, why my child?" One mother had placed a cold towel over Marie's eyes. Another mother was preparing food for the three younger children. I stood there in silence, wondering what I could do. We were all struggling with bits and pieces of this tragedy.

"Where's Marie?" Albert asked as he glanced around the small living room, which looked more crowded with the seven extra women being there. He rushed over to the chair near the dining room, knelt down, and hugged his wife.

"What happened, baby?" Albert softly uttered.

"They shot him!" Marie cried out loud. "They wouldn't stop him without shooting him first. Oh, Albert what can we do?

"Who shot Bobby, Honey?" Albert was rubbing her hands, oblivious to all of us watching.

"One of the cops," Marie sighed deep again. "I heard Bobby calling to me from the corner. They shot him."

Everything was too quiet for all day Friday. Saturday evening, not one teenager was allowed outside "on the streets." Sunday, few ventured out to attend their local church. People moved around like zombies, not uttering a word. Few conversations were taking place. We all felt helpless. Marie came out of her grief a few days later. She called on the phone, asking me to come over to be with her for a little while. I lived directly across the street. Once we sat down, she started expressing her thoughts.

"Eleanor, we got to do something before somebody else's child gets killed." She sat there drained of hope.

"Yeah," I whispered. "I've been wondering what could be done. I would hate to see this happen to anybody else.

"You're good with folks, Eleanor." Marie sat on the edge of her sofa. "Can't you go talk to some of those big people you know? You know what I'm talking about? Like the Mayor?

"The Mayor didn't shot anybody," I sadly remarked. "Sounds more like a police problem to me. I think the real thing is they don't know any of us. They don't know we love our kids, try to make them behave, and one little thing happens: BOOM! They're gone." We both sat there quietly feeling helpless without any clear thoughts. What could be the next step? I stood up, stretched, and told Marie I had to go before the kids came home from school.

I remain preoccupied the rest of the day wondering what, if anything, could be done. I became anxious. I certainly did not want any of our five sons shot by the police. I decided the next morning that I would take the Third Street bus to downtown San Francisco and talk to the Police

Chief. This was still upsetting the families, revealing a sense of hopelessness.

Once at the Police Station, I went straight to the Information Desk and asked for the Chief.

"Could you tell me the reason you want to see the Chief?" the receptionist asked.

"I prefer to tell him myself if he is here." I held my head a trifle higher, determined to be heard.

"Please have a seat," she indicated rather dryly.

I sat there for at least fifteen minutes, feeling a bit nervous.

"Good afternoon. My name is LT. Dan Anderson. What can we do for you today?" He extended his right hand towards me.

"I want to meet the Chief," I said very rapidly. "We have five sons and we don't want anything to happen to them."

"Where do you live?" The LT. seemed interested in my comments.

"We live near Candlestick Park, in the Alice Griffith Projects," I said firmly.

"I'll see if the Chief is free." The LT. left the room, and returned seconds later. "Come with me. What's your name?

"Mrs. Curry."

We entered this large office. Behind the biggest desk I had ever seen sat a robust man with flaming red hair. Chief Thomas C. LT. Anderson offered me a seat and he sat down beside me.

"Hello there, young lady," the Chief said in a baritone voice. "What can we do for you today?

"I thought I should talk to you regarding keeping my sons from being shot by some Police Officer, whether on purpose or by accident." I paused, suddenly realizing I was actually talking with one of the highest ranking people in law enforcement. "When I was a little girl, my mother used to tell us, 'if you ever run into trouble with any bad people, call the blue coats.' I later found out 'blue coats' meant policemen. So I'm here to see if anything can be done to halt some of this dangerous stuff happening to our kids."

"How many sons are you talking about and how old are they?" The Chief seemed sincerely interested.

"We have five sons, with the oldest son being ten years old."

The Chief laughed out loud with a twinkle in his eyes.

"Well, Mrs. Curry," as he interlocked his fingers on the desk, "you have a legitimate concern. Let me think this over. One of my Officers will reach you right away (he was flipping through his calendar schedule)." "How about in a week?"

We each stood up, nodding in agreement. The following week I received a call from the LT. The Chief wanted to know if I'd like to serve on the newly-formed Police-Community Relations Board, effective in the fall of the year (September 1961). I said, "YES!" Things began to change.

Monthly meetings were held at the local Recreation Center and in some of our homes. LT. Anderson was assigned to our area. We learned of various laws that would protect our children. The Police began to learn the names of the different families and started recognizing the teenagers in our neighborhood. I was chosen to speak at the Police Academy about how to treat our families with respect.

I recall one session when the subject was on 'Leadership in Poor Neighborhoods.'

"Poor people need to have some leaders right among them, but that doesn't exist!" a veteran policeman emphatically stated. "Normally we're called when things have escalated, become very emotional, and completely out of control. Who do we contact to avoid trouble?" He asked the fellow officers to think of solutions to protect innocent citizens.

When my turn came to speak later that afternoon, I wrote three leaders' names on the blackboard: Judge Joseph Kent, Attorney Terrie Franklin, and President Eleanor Curry. Immediately the officers started whispering, "Who is this President Curry?" Once it became apparent I was President of our local church, a lively discussion was generated concerning protecting innocent people, especially in low-income neighborhoods.

There were several months of such communications and the holiday season was approaching. Right before Thanksgiving, one of the Officers from the Police Commission came to see me.

"Mrs. Curry, our Officers voted this year to select this neighborhood to receive the collections for any low-income people you choose. You do not have to give the names of the families. We hope you would know which families are in the most need." He actually saluted, shook my hand, and left.

I thanked him, rushed into the kitchen, spread hundreds of dollars on the kitchen table and began writing the names of the specific families. My husband, now home from work, saw the money.

"What are you doing? Where did you get all that money from?" He asked wide-eyed. Once I explained what had happen, he asked quickly? "Did you put our family on the list?"

"Of course not, silly, you have a job," I said, still counting. He simply laughed and told me "You're the silly one." We had a great holiday for many families with over $700.00 in donations. We all sent Thank You notes.

Do you think such communications could work in 2010?

PART THREE: SAN MATEO, CALIFORNIA

San Mateo seems to be the ideal place to raise a family. We bought our first house in 1965, with one teenage daughter and five sons still living at home. It was a small, with two bedrooms and one bathroom on the first floor, and a large dilapidated attic. It became obvious we had to renovate the building while living there.

11 RACIAL INTEGRATION IN SAN MATEO

When Dr. Martin Luther King spoke during the March on Washington in 1963, he was electrifying to the entire nation with his "I Have a Dream" speech. I sat alone in my living room mesmerized. I jumped up clapping at the end of his presentation. I immediately wondered to myself, 'What can I do to support Dr. King's movement?' We knew that, even in California, things should be better for African-American citizens.

Here's what happened in one northern California City.

These pictorial documents below were presented at the San Mateo County Historical Society Museum in Redwood City, California.

Local Newspapers

In and About San Mateo County

- Charles Thrower, Publisher of *The Peninsula Bulletin* (a weekly newspaper)
- Vera Graham, Columnist for *The San Mateo Times* (a daily newspaper)

While the major newspapers described the events surrounding the civil rights movement, the local smaller newspapers covered the San Mateo Elementary School District efforts weekly.

12 CO-PARENTS CONCEPT, WHAT, WHERE AND WHY.

The Co-parent concept came as the result of the 279 students who were taking buses to the 23 schools in the elementary school district. Ms. Nancy Barker, a teacher from the local pre-nursery school brought the idea to the attention of the staff. After a month of weekly meetings, held separately between the black parents and white parents, school by school, both groups of parents were joined together. It was so successful. It became the heart of the district's plan. When the project was evaluated a year later, one of the black parents gave her opinion saying, "It's good. At first, the white families were scared we were coming, and we were scared were going."

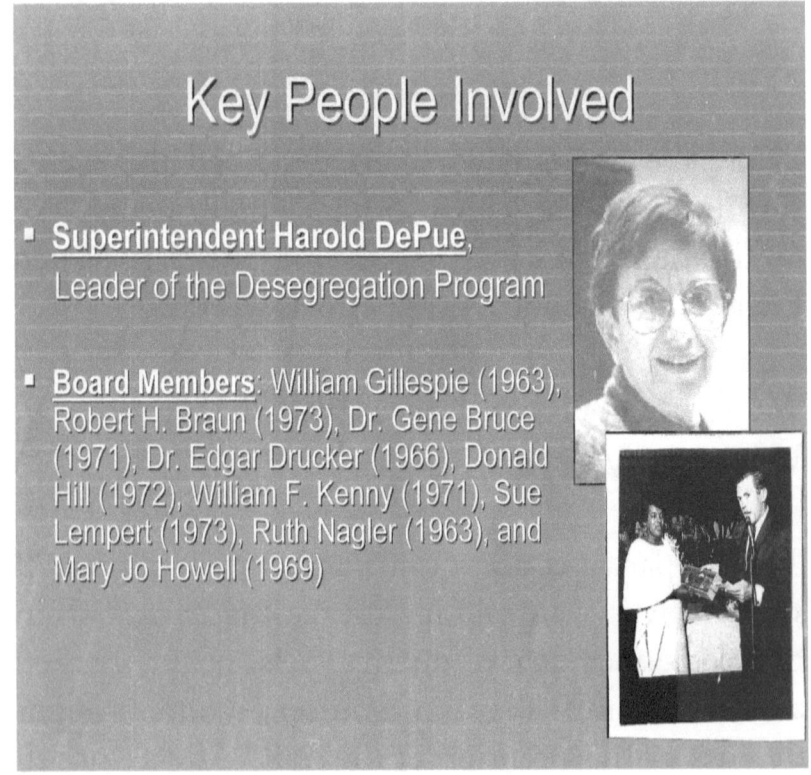

Key People Involved

■ **Superintendent Harold DePue**, Leader of the Desegregation Program

■ **Board Members**: William Gillespie (1963), Robert H. Braun (1973), Dr. Gene Bruce (1971), Dr. Edgar Drucker (1966), Donald Hill (1972), William F. Kenny (1971), Sue Lempert (1973), Ruth Nagler (1963), and Mary Jo Howell (1969)

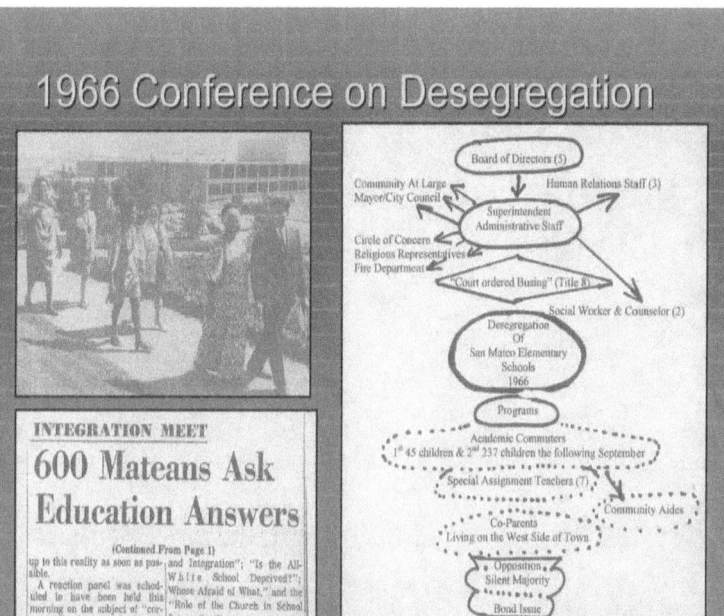

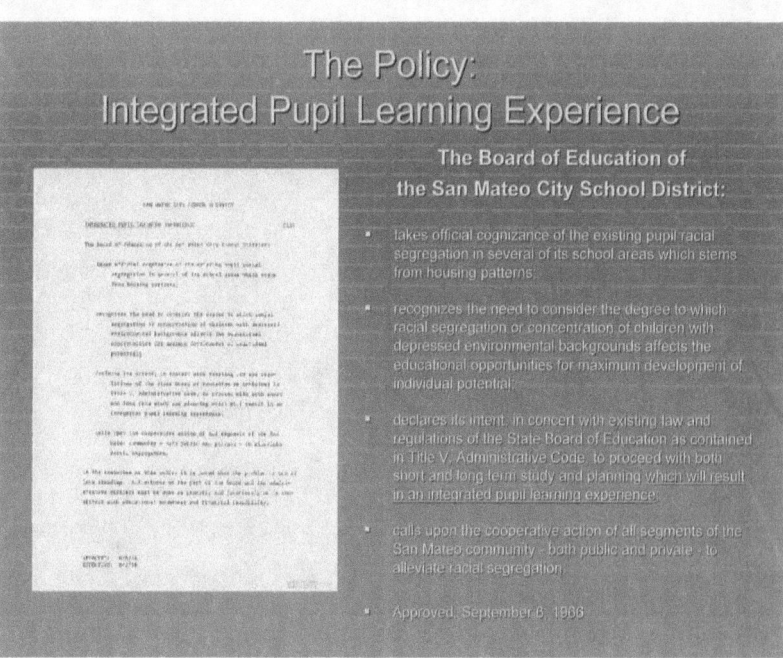

The First Day

- 45 kids were supposed to be bused on the first day, including Paul Curry

- One protester – James Tormey, Jr.

- Bond Measure concern

- Safety concerns

- What's most important?

- What happened?

Involved Civic Leaders, Parents, and Volunteers: 1966-1978

Mayor Roy Archibald, Jack Alexander, Helen Barfield, Dorothy Bates, Barbara Bibbs, Dorothy Biscoe, Evelyn Blodgett, Carrie Bratton, Nancy Barker, Rev. Benjamin Brooks, Alfred Brown, Rev. James Brown, Dan Belnap, Rev. George P. Carter, Della Conner, Rev. Rufus Cooper, Lottie Crumb, Betty Curtis, Marlene DeLancie, Bernice Donat, Frobie Ernest, Andrew Field, Sue Garratt, Stephen Gehre, Dorothy Greene, Ola Mae Green, Sidney & Loretta Hall, Rev. Alanson Higbie, Freemon & Myzie Hollands, Leah Cotton, Dr. Zelte Crawford, Dr. James & Evelyn Hutchinson, Fred Howell, Kumi Ishida, Irene Ikeda, Ann Ito, Zelma Jackson, Rosanne levitt, Arthur lillard, Marshall & Mary lytle, Frances Matthews, Dorothy Mays, Velma McCrary, Jean Melcher, Lt. Thurman McGinnis, Rev. Paul Mitchell, Margie Morris, Richard Morgan, Masako Nagumo, Evelyn Neely, Eliza Nelson, Curtis & Jean Norwood, Gladys Norton, Marian Newgard, Nan Palmer, Lucy Cupp Pickens, Dan & Majorie Portrait, Rev. Donald Pyne, Rabbi Sanford Rosen, Harryette Rucker, Rev. Herbert Van Meter, Pat Olson, Patricia Ray, Eva Rhodes, Jean Robinson, Trish Ronald, Emily Scholnic, Joan Sheldon, Milton Shields, Maraget Segal, Rev. William Semple, Jessie Staton, James Tormey, Jr. Hy Tsukamoto, Evelyn Trotter, Colleen Trouse, Jill Wakeman, Jane Weidman, Althea Wiggins, Mary Williams and Joann Witt

Staff and Teachers Involved:
1966-1978

- **School District Staff**: Kay Armstrong, Dan Broussard, Freddie Buchanan, Eleanor Curry, Ida Gilbert, Gus Guichard, Colleen Hausler, Eula Mae Hicks, John Hiler, Thomas Konno, Claire Mack, Earl Neilson, Ella Phillips, Erma Prothro, Johnnie May Robinson, Hannah Shields, Eureka Utsumi, Florence Yoshiwara and Naomi Yum

- **Teachers**: Ernestine Mazola, Fannie Merida, Evelyn Taylor, Velia Pedrotti, Virginia Seminoff, Bonnie Tabak and Doris Vallon

- **Principals**: All the principals in the district supported the policy set forth by the Board.

- **San Mateo Elementary Teachers Association**: The Association maintained stability in preparing the teachers for this historical movement.

The City of San Mateo and Beyond

- San Mateo Union High School District:
  - Dr. Leon Lessinger, Superintendent
  - Staff: Charles Douglas, Mildred Swann, Ike Tribble, Edward Valeau and Roger Winston

- Sequoia Union High School District:
  - Dr. Harry Reynolds, Superintendent
  - Staff: Bobbie Arnold, Sarah Boyd, Dorothy Burnside, Ana Dalavalade, Mary Frazier, Lois Freemon, Katie McCall, Vera Patrick, Dr. Andrew and Viola White

- East Palo Alto Community Leaders:
  - Dr. Harry Reynolds, Superintendent
  - Staff: Bobbie Arnold, Sarah Boyd, Dorothy Burnside, Ana Dalavalade, Mary Frazier, Lois Freemon, Katie McCall, Vera Patrick, Dr. Andrew and Viola White

- San Mateo County Supervisors

Note: This is a partial listing of key individuals that set the fundamental moral support to ensure all the children were treated equal during these turbulent times.

San Mateo County Public Services

- **Community College District**
  - Chancellor Glenn Smith, leader of College of San Mateo, Skyline College and Canada College
  - Staff: Eric Gattman and Dr. Zelte Crawford

- **Office of Education**
  - Dr. Floyd Gonella, Dr. Cecil Reeves, Joyce Reeves, Carol Slavick and Doris Ward

- **Human Relations Commission**
  - James Forrest, Executive Director
  - Human Relations Staff

Others

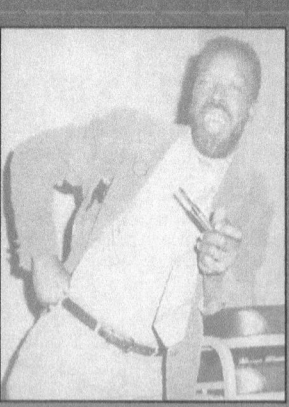

- Robert C. Jacobs

- Ben Parks

- Kenneth Strom

Brown vs. The Board of Education was declared law in 1954. Twelve years later, the City of San Mateo set policies to desegregate the San Mateo Elementary School District. An Inter-group Relations Specialist was hired to develop the District's integration plan. The budget was approved to develop a Human Relations Department.

The first 45 students were bused from the North Central side of San Mateo to several schools on the West side of San Mateo in February 1967, without any racial incidents. In September 1967, an additional 267 students became academic commuters.

San Mateo Elementary School District (SMESD)

When I was hired to be a Human Relations Specialist for the SMESD, once I read the job description I realized it was more than just an ordinary job. The key role states, 'to service all of the students in the 23 public schools with the desegregation concept'. The Supreme Court decision, -Brown vs. the Board of Education/1954, ordered all public schools across the country to integrate. Court ordered busing was a major tool used to implement this order.

While some of the residents protested against desegregating the District, it was not a large outcry. The main items centered on a school bond issue on the ballot, and some parents fearing for the safety of their children being bused to the west side of town.

None of the fears became a reality. The school board voted unanimously to desegregate the schools in 1966.

Twelve years after Brown vs. The Board of Education decree, we are moving into uncharted waters in this northern city. We immediately set up a series of home meetings on both sides of town. Six weeks later the first 45 students were bused to several schools without any negative incidents. Next, another 340 students were bused throughout the district. In 1968 the final group of students was integrated into the 23 public schools.

How did such smooth transitions take place? The entire city of San Mateo embraced the theory of caring for all its students. The SMESD took a precise leadership stance, keeping the surrounding environments up to date with the numerous steps. Several private residents created special ideas to help focus the District's efforts.

SMESD: Superintendent Hal Depue, a man of compassion and vision, spearheads the Administrative Transfer Plan. Gus Guichard, Intergroup Educational Specialist, is hired to present the Administrative Transfer Plan. Guichard indicates in a Progress Report saying, "The relative ease with which this 'district' has accomplished its success is a reflection of the planning, dedication and vigilance of school personnel, parents and other interested community persons. This program report will only attempt to point out some significant elements which contribute to continuing success or which identify present problems or predict future ones".

According to Guichard, the areas critical to the plan covered Transportation, Enrollment and Pupil Reception, School-Parent contact, Parent-Teacher Association, Parent Survey, Staff Participation(heavy emphasis on Staff Orientation and Communication), Teachers on Special Assignment and Teacher –Aide assignment , as "School Community Worker". Such a comprehensive plan was vital to the total staff and especially the teachers, who had the major contact with the new students.

Teachers on Special Assignments: Seven teachers have been assigned to the 18 schools receiving the new students. The teachers are under joint supervision of the Intergroup Education Department and the Department of Instruction. The teachers were chosen for their experience and insight they could bring to helping individual students in remedial work, working with their parents and by encouraging the classroom teachers to deeper perception of cultural differences, in areas designated by the principal. Bonnie Tabak, one of the seven teachers offered a top notch suggestion beyond the norm of her regular work. Bonnie said, "Let's have traveling multi-cultural dinners. We'll need several people to volunteer their homes. The homes will be close together so the guests can walk to each house. First house will have appetizers, the next, soups, plus salads, next, the main dinner course and finally, the desserts. We can have these gatherings once a month, inviting all the teachers, parents and friends from a defined middle school site. This way, we'll get to know each other better in a relaxed atmosphere". The event began two months later and became a large success.

Teacher Aides: Although teacher aides have been involved on a part-time basis to help teachers with overcrowded classrooms, another role is eminent with the transfer students. The aides become "School Community Workers", whose primary job is to keep the channels of communication open between disadvantage parents and the individual school or teacher. The community worker opens brand new doors for the hard-to-reach parents, but also their own families as they discover more about how schools handle behavior problems, areas of testing, and extra-curricular activities. It has been an enlighten point to realize so much was accomplished due to a spirit of apparent willingness.

Clear understanding was developing rather than 'put-downs', racial intimidation and prejudicial stereotypical behavior. It appears to be due more to a lack of experience, insight and exact knowledge, rather than an indication of deep-seated intolerance or discrimination.

Parent-Teacher Association: The traditional P.T.A. Coordinating Committee proved most valuable due to the keen interest in sharing of common problems and solutions regardless of the ethnicity of the students. The important feedback to and from each local school P.T. A. President minimized possible outburst of behavior as all the students learned habits of adjusting to each other.

Staff Orientation/ communication: Effective communication is an absolute requirement whenever any transitional shifts take place among large groups. A maximum of 58 volunteer persons representing every group that worked in the school system spent a weeklong orientation workshop (Breaking the Barriers to Communication) during the last week in the month of August. This set the opportunity to investigate the quality and methods on inter-personal communication, to explore these techniques in sensitivity training groups ("T-groups) and through lecture-discussions formats. The evaluation indicated that the sensitivity training was the most significant and helpful part of the workshop. Each teacher present was ready to encourage and share this type information with the faculty at the school site.

Minority Problem Committee: Simultaneously the community at large and prominent civic leaders along with the Intergroup Education Specialist began frequent meeting with its Minority Problems Committee Team. Those attending 98% of their time in the sessions were the following:

Jack Alexander	Kay Armstrong
Evelyn Blodgett	Alfred Brown
Eleanor Curry	Marlene DeLancie
Dr. Edward Feldman	Mary Jo Howell
Ann Ito	Thomas H. Konno
Jean Melcher	Richard Morgan
Alfred Morris	Jean Robinson
Eureka Utsumi	Jill Wakeman.

There were important discussions concerning kindergarten children, Head Start programs and how the integrated learning should promote better academic performance. This is viewed as one way to not have more young people from minority population in prisons who, have been segregated and denied an adequate education.

Circle of Concern: The Circle of Concern is an inter-racial group of church women with vital interest and timelines to be shared with other persons. The film "A Time for Burning", features the efforts of an all-white in Berkeley and the attempt to have inter-racial meetings with a near- by Negro Lutheran Church. The Reverend spear-heading the documentary, as a result of the controversy over his project, was asked to resign. The Circle of Concern held monthly meetings to give individuals the opportunity to vent any issues which centered on racial matters. While the majority of the time people were civil, at other times topics brought out hidden emotions from all sides in attendance. The ideal message became "Let us agree to disagree agreeably".

Marian Newgard, Private Citizen: "When my son Craig, was in high school, he had many friends of different racial groups. Most of all he did not understand why the black students had such a hard time in the academics and was so good in sports. I decided to invite a few of them to our home during lunchtime. They appeared bright and well mannered. I met some of their families. One day Craig was killed in a car accident. Our family was devastated. I thought about Craig and all the new exciting people he had brought into my life. To honor him I created the CRAIG NEWGARD AWARD for black students only. This motivated the black students to study harder to win the award.

Marian Newgard held an annual afternoon tea every January, at her home, bringing together civic leaders, educators, parents and many friends to enjoy each others' differences and company.

13 SAN MATEO COUNTY'S TURBULENT TIMES

San Mateo City Government: Early 1968, with the Transfer Plan in high gear, San Mateo Mayor Roy Archibald officially encourages more than thirty additional organizations to join discussions to improve racial relations. The issues were beyond the transfer plans to the problems of jobs, education and housing for minorities. San Mateo has a "chance" to solve the problems leading to racial tensions; therefore all ideas shall be explored with implementation where possible. Mayor Archibald was available to ensure his staff was ready to implement the necessary laws to seek fairness, and equality.

San Mateo Congregation Church: The local leaders of the various churches received a letter from one of the clergyman asking this question. "Are we not all confronted with this question of our role as current leaders of the Judeo-Christian tradition and its ministry of reconciliation? We are inviting two laymen to join the efforts of several ministers to consider these matters as they affect San Mateo, Burlingame, Hillsborough and Millbrae. We feel the destructive effect of racial separation calls concerned Churchmen to "come together "to gain information and mutual support for our common task." Rev. Herbert Van Meter, Congregational Church of San Mateo

Eva Rhodes: An unexpected idea from one of the employees of the Mayor came from Eva Rhodes, Staff at the Martin Luther King Jr., Community Center. In her own words:

"We have many African American children that are actually bi-racial. Their skin color, if extremely light makes some people think they are 'white' causing them to suffer another type of harassment. As I observed the problems of this group and hear them tell me stories of boredom, hopelessness and few jobs for them, I knew there had to be another way. Unfortunately, drugs were taking a devastating affect on a small percentage of the black teenagers.

Every time we had individual talks or group discussions, I sounded like a broken record; 'stay off the corner, don't sell drugs, stay in school, run from trouble, what are you doing to yourself?' When my own teenagers begin to talk off their future dreams, a light bulb hit my brain. JOIN THE ARMY! Honey, I called the Recruiting Office that very next day. We set up weekly pep talks. The teens were excited, showing up and listening intently. They were on the road to a second chance. Many joined the service. Yet due to minor violations, over 29 could not be accepted, because they had driving tickets unpaid, or a drivers' license had expired."

One young man joined the Air Force, sent overseas and loved being in the service. Months later he received a pass to return home for a week-end. He was overjoyed. Once back in California, getting off the airplane, reaching for his passport, it was not there. He had left it at the base. Meantime, Carolyn Bailey-Thomas, a prominent Real Estate Broker living in Sacramento, was on her way to pick her son up. Once arriving, The Recruitment Officer, explained, he cannot be released without proper identification."

"What can we do?" Carolyn whispered desperately, "He only has the week-end."

"Where did you live before your current address?"

"We lived in San Mateo, near the San Francisco Airport. My son was part of the JOIN THE ARMY program."

"Are you kidding me? You must know a woman named Eva Rhodes from MLK Community Center. She saved quite a few people, both young men and women. That's enough I.D. for your son".

When Eva heard this incident, she said smiling, "As my dad always said, there are no CREEDS without DEEDS".

Racial Conflicts in High Schools: San Mateo County is comprised of 21 Cities. Other cities within the County had begun to implement Transfer plans too, mainly in the public high schools. After 258 years of segregated laws, it is impossible to imagine every single person never having any racial tensions, both blacks and whites. The complexities of race have constantly been exposed to the extremes that block meaningful dialogues. The situation I'm most familiar with occurs at San Mateo High School. I'm serving as the local Human Relations Commission Chair. One of my sons had been hit in the head with a chair. The Principal had called the Police Department and had the white student sent to juvenile hall to avoid a riot. A Mass meeting was held at the MLK Center that same night. Over 250 People attends.

A young adult heavy set cinnamon colored Black man with microphone in his hand saying, "I hear to tell you right now, there'll be no more running over our people (Blacks) if we hear of it. You need to know tonight we came to stop abuses of..." Someone, another thinner black man, came to the speaker with a note. They talked a few seconds. The speaker stares at the audience, saying in the same booming voice, "I know most of you here are not students. What happen to the students has to be straightening out by them. All of you over thirty years old can please leave now!"

I couldn't believe my ears. I wondering who these people are and where did they come. They must not live in San Mateo. Next, I couldn't believe my eyes. The majority of the people quietly left the Center. I sat there astonished at their departure. The thinner man glances over the remaining crowd. He stops when he sees me. He says something to the first guy. He looks directly at me (near the back door), saying" Hey you, I said everybody over thirty leave NOW!" I looked behind me never moving.

"You, near the back door. How old are you?"

"Twenty-nine years old". The crowd roared with laughter, with someone shouting, "Let her stay, she's crazy."Staying there prepared me for helping save the students the next day.

I arrived at the High School the next morning. The principal wants me to handle the assembled student body of approximately 1200 people. The Police officers have the school ground surrounded. The purpose is to let the students try to figure out what had happen and how to get peace back on campus. The students were very emotionally charged, angry, full of blame and ready to strike out at anyone nearby. Whenever a student came to the mike, others would shout out saying, "That's a lie. You are stupid. You know you're making that story up".

"Wait a minute", I gaveled for order, and "We need to get ourselves under control. Repeat this statement after me. When I count to three say these words. Every man thinks he's right in his mind, but God ponders our heart, 1, 2, 3". All 1200 Students shouts back the verse. We started over. We were engaged in serious conversation from 9 A.M. to Noon. A Police Officer brought me the message that all weapons had been collected. I could close the assembly. No casualties. Peace has been restored.

Until Justice Rolls down like a Mighty Stream

DR. MLK, JR.

1967-2009: Forty-two years ago, an entire community in San Mateo, California stepped up for equality and justice. More stories can be told regarding these momentous years. The period of racial integration in the 1960s and 1970s is one of the different themes now preserved in our local history.

How does one measure any success of a movement? Let's call this a positive landscape shift.

Where are those Transfer students now? Please enjoy a partial listing of some of those students and career choices.

Carl Brown, Brown Construction Company

Dennis Caines, Attorney

Ronald Cannon, International Opera Singer

David Curry, Home Improvement Specialist

Paul Curry, Business Consultant/Adult Care Giver, Construction/Retail Sales

William Curry, Real Estate Broker

Dexter Currington, Police Officer

Ava Davis, Property Manager, Antioch, California

John-John Davis, Renovates Automobiles, Stockton, California

Marla Davis, Culinary Chef, San Leandro, California

Jacqueline Gilbert, Political Consultant, Ministry

Dennis Haysbert, Actor

Cheryl Hollands, Child Care Provider

Phyllis Farris, lives in Richmond, CA.

Jeffery Jackson, Ministry Leader

Felicia Jones, County Government Employee

George Kubota, lives in Hawaii

Steve Kubota, lives in Hawaii

Vicki Mack, Gospel Centric Founder

Leslie Mack, Consultant, Culinary Planner

Kelly Mack, Dentist, National Reserves

Angela Page, Director of MLK Community Center, San Mateo California

Eva Rhodes, Consumer College, Sutter Hospital, Assistant to the Dean, Sacramento, California

Kathi Rhodes, Recruiter of VSP (Vision Specialist Programs), Sacramento, California

Thomas Rhodes, Air Force, Captain of the Marines. Director of CHAPS LAB. Sacramento, California

Walter 'Wally' Rhodes, CISCO Assembly Systems. Engineer. Sacramento, California

Elonda Slade Robinson, Sports Advisor

Rhonda Robinson, Government Employee, Woodbridge, Virginia

Brian Swann, Dentist

William Calvin Swann, Manager of. U.C. University, Parking facility, Seattle, Washington

Lynn Swann, T.V. National Sports Announcer

Hope Whipple, Director, Community Service Center

Janice Wheeler Crumb, Patient Accountant, San Francisco General Hospital

Note: A goodly portion of the Transfer students are of the Oriental population. Little is known about their careers.

TRIANGULAR
APPROACH TEAM

Every society shapes educational institutions to perpetuate its culture, values, traditions and way of life. Ours is a changing society and problems are ever changing. Changes are more rapid today than ever before, thereby creating their own new problems as they surface. This rapidly further tends to create need which are outstripping the resources to meet them; i.e. introducing Black History units into curriculum without adequate research; formulating Black Dignity and multiethnic classes without enough adults to man the courses.

In our endeavor to prepare children for a viable, dynamic society, we are guided by our commitment to an integrated society. We envision a society in which people strive for the idealism of a better life not only for themselves, but especially for their children and grandchildren. This better life cannot be earned in isolation; especially in our highly technical and mobile society.

Prepared by: Kay Armstrong, School Social Worker

              Eleanor Curry, School-Community Relations Advisor

              Thomas H. Konno, School-Community Counselor

ARTICLES REPRESENTING ACTUAL WORK AND PROGRAMS

WORKING WITH COMMUNITY
by Eleanor Williams

TEN KEY BRIDGES

ONE: Define the Leadership. Start with the Leadership. Stay with the Leadership.

TWO: Never make Promises you cannot keep.

THREE: Listen 3 times more than you talk; to Understand; to Clarify; to Seek Decisions.

FOUR: Discuss Regulations, Risks and Rules.

FIVE: Remain Factual, Flexible and Friendly.

SIX: Do not Pre-judge.

SEVEN: Second the Motions, don't make them.

EIGHT: Expect Setbacks, Surprises and Success.

NINE: Influence the Behavior through Praise, Partnerships and Principles.

TEN: Know what you have Finished, Celebrate, Begin Again!

COUNTY OF SAN MATEO
HOUSING DIVISION
262 HARBOR BLVD., BLDG A
BELMONT, CA 94002
(415) 802-5050

KEYS OF LEADERSHIP

Love = seeking the best for all human beings and creatures of God left to our care.

Earnest = pay attention by handling small details, the big details emerge.

Advocate = finding a need, and filling it for yourself and others.

Discipline = do your part, encourage others to do theirs.

Elder = learn from anyone older than yourself, wisdom is stored with elders.

Responsible = I am my Word. Do what you say, or let someone know when you can't.

Sincerity = seek truth, value time, and speak the truth.

Hope = start every day with fresh eyes, and look for new possiblities each day.

Iinclusion = be careful of images, of distorition, or misconception. Seek good ideas.

Persevere = learn your purpose and master one major subject. Avoid being scattered.

"If you desire to be a leader, it can be done. It is a wonderful journey, because you're helping others as you grow yourself."

From Segregated St. Louis, Missouri
To Suburban San Mateo County, California

Eleanor Curry is a Civic Community Leader,
a wife, mother, grandmother and great grand mother.
She loves to promote family values.
She is one of ten outstanding women
in the State of California (1995) named by the
Commission on the Status of Women.

SOUL FOOD/A CULTURAL BLESSING

By EleanorWilliams-Curry

So much of this segregation bit is in the mind. People aren't just segregating themselves too. Like, how many of you have ever tasted hominy grits? Black-eyed peas? Chitlins? No law against it. You try tomorrow, and I guarantee you won't turn one shade darker. It doesn't make sense-prejudice against foods. I mean, I've been eating gefilte fish for years even before I knew Sammy Davis, Jr.!

Dick Gregory/from the Back of the Bus/1962

When Dr. Martin Luther King, Jr., James Baldwin, and Dick Gregory to name a few, were attacking the walls of segregation in the early 60's, some others of us were speaking about the daily living of Black America.

One day, when I was 15 years old, I asked my mother "What is this thing we call 'Soul Food'? She looked puzzled at first. Than she laughed, put her hands on her hips and stated, "Honey, It's the way we cook and what we have been forced to eat." She was excited about explaining to me the depths of the Depression (1929), how not to get upset cause you're hungry and how they had to search for food.

"We had to find and cook food to hold our body and soul together. I've been cooking ever since the minute my eyes cleared the top of the big black iron stove in Mama's kitchen. I believe I was about nine years old. Although my degree was in nursing, we all had to learn to cook. Your Uncles, King Bob, Woodie, and Cecil worked in the white restaurants, cooking on the side, after their main job. On the weekend the marketplace in St. Louis would sell us food the white people would not eat. Mama would go and beg for the butcher to give her bags of Chitlins. We got 10 pounds in buckets for .25cents. We cleaned this part of the pig for hours. Next came the seasoning of whole onions, pickling spice, garlic plus salt and pepper. Cooking chitlins takes about 4 hours. If any were leftover, we would prepare an egg batter, dip the pieces in flour and make French Fried Chitlins." Talk about something original and good. Today Chitlins are a delicacy. The price is $6.00 for 10 pounds (1944). This is one way we would prepare the food so you couldn't recognize it. We loved to make the scraps of food become our own banquets. I'm not talking about the slavery days. I'm talking about right now."

"When are you going to teach me how to cook Soul Food?" I asked interested in starting.
"Never, she said emphatic, "You keep getting those good grades, get your education and you can read cookbooks".

One thing I discovered once I finished high school, the recipes my mother and uncles prepared were not in any cookbooks.

My first lesson on how to cook 'Soul Food' came from Ruth, my sister-in-law. After being married to my husband for about four months she calls me.

"Girl, what on earth are you feeding my brother?" Ruth bluntly inquired.

"He doesn't eat very much". I respond, rather surprised, "Mostly I open a can of Chicken noodle soup and have some crackers."

"WHAT?" Ruth shouts, Girl you better learn how to cook, before my brother leaves you. He comes over here every day after work. He acts like he is being starved to death. Come over here tomorrow so I can teach you how to cook."

The next place lessons came from the African American churches in our neighborhood. The Sisters could cook. They are famous for their home cooked meals, especially Fried Chicken. They cooked to celebrate the good times. They bought chickens, cooked the chickens and made you order the chicken dinners for any cause. When they needed to raise money for the church, get ready to order a Chicken dinner. Many an African American Church was built because the Sisters of the church sold those chicken dinners. That was before Kentucky Fried Chicken.

Whether we live in the ghetto, the city or the suburbs, all black people identify with 'Soul Food'. We believe our food heals our bodies. The delicious recipes from our 'Soul Food' memory banks are so plentiful, we often swap recipes on the telephone. We give the food names, like Aunt Adele's hogshead cheese, Aunt Bonnie's pound cake, Uncle Frank's red beans and rice, Aunt Brenda's gumbo, Papa Curry's supreme smothered cabbage and Bill's 'hush your mouth' Bar-B-Q ribs. The traditional sweet potato pie has become Mama Curry's sweet potato pie. Wait until you make and taste this 'melt right in your mouth' dish. After making 1500 pies over 40 years, here's MAMA CURRY'S SWEET POTATO PIE:

One 9-inch pie yields 8 thin servings

1 can of sweet potatoes
½ cup white sugar
¼ cup dark brown sugar
1 egg
¼ cup of evaporated milk
1 tablespoon soft butter or margin
2 teaspoon of nutmeg
3 teaspoon of cinnamon
1 package of frozen pie crust (follow directions)

Preheat the oven to 375 F. Take out piecrust from package and set aside.
Drain the sweet potatoes. Mash with eggbeater until smooth. Add both sugars. Crack the egg and separate the white from the yolk. Put the egg white in the freezer for a brief minute. Place the yolk only, in the batter, continue to beat the mixer until smooth. Stir in the milk, butter and spices. Continue to mix. Remove beaters from mixer, rinse and return to mixer. Remove egg white from freezer. Beat whites with mixer until foamy. Add two tablespoons of sugar. Beat until white peaks take form. Remove eggbeaters. Fold white peaks into the sweet potato batter. Pour into thawed piecrust, Sprinkle nutmeg on top of pie. Bake at 375 F. for 28 to 30 minutes. Test with a toothpick to ensure firmness of batter. Remove and let cool for 20 minutes.

HAPPY BLACK HISTORY MONTH CELEBRATION!

-2-

2-14-02

TIME HAPPENS DAILY

Time. Think 24 hours.
Time. We all have the same 24 hours.
Time. How are you spending your 24 brief hours?

We waste time by procrastination. It seems easier to put it off until tomorrow. Tomorrow is too far away. Why not do it today?

Most recently in the business management world a very popular book was published "First Things First" by Stephen R. Covey. Several concepts are raised by Covey. His thinking centers on the difference between knowing what's important and what's urgent. Can you put people ahead of schedules? Spending the time on the job might not be as important as being with the children. Are you trying to figure out the gap between what needs to be done vs. what you really want to do? How can you spend quality time with family, friends and the job without feeling overwhelmed?

I wonder what Jesus would say about how we use our time today. We ponder putting "First Things First". Jesus had the same issue. What did he do? First of all, Jesus was a balanced person. He prayed daily. He talked with his family. He talked to the woman at the well and, of course, other people one on one. He trained the disciples. He was a master teacher. He loved the church and its fellowship. How did he do all of this? I venture to say he set priorities! That's right: he knew what to do first.

Look at our present experiences. Here I am attempting to juggle several issues every single day. What comes first that matters to you and those you care about? I have discovered this works for me:
First I pray to God, early in the morning and around noon and every night.
Second place belongs to my spouse.
Third are the children, plus other family members.
Fourth are friends, people who encourage us, relax us and generate different thoughts.
Fifth is work. We need to be there doing our best service.
Sixth is worship, not for just us, but for God and others. Recall a great handshake, a hug, a sincere smile.
Seventh is rest. Yes, that mighty habit God knew we must have called 'rest'.

24 hours of planning sent me back to college. 24 hours of good living brought me joy. How are you spending your 24 hours?

Eleanor Williams-Curry
2/25/05

ARE YOU HEALTHY?

Health is God's gift to human beings. Health is wealth. Health is mind, body and soul in harmony.

Where did you learn about being healthy? Why do we have so many people who are ill? When did we realize things were getting out of hand concerning our health?
How can we reverse the trend of people getting sicker and sicker? What authorities do we turn to eliminate disease and think wellness? Why are employees rewarded with sick days off from work instead of wellness days? What should be the top priority in the health field? Should it be medical institutions, alternative medicines or chiropractic and wellness care services? Why not seek the best health plan from various sources?

Webster's Dictionary defines health as:

1. The general condition of the body or mind with reference to soundness and vigor.
2. Soundness of body or mind; freedom from disease or aliment.
3. A polite or complimentary wish for a person's health, happiness, etc., especially as a toast
4. Vigor, vitality: economic health.

Most of the things associated with health concepts appear to focus on a multitude of diseases. Just think about every day life, when you meet someone. Have you heard any of these various comments when you ask this simple question?
"How are you today?" Here are a few responses.

"Fair to middling."
"A cold is trying to catch me."
"I've had better days. My legs just gave out."
" My back is acting up again."
"The weather is making my arthritis stiffen my joints."
"I went to the doctor to get my medicine. Honey, even if the medicine cures me, the price will kill me."
"There's so much stuff on the drug stores' shelves I don't know what to pick up. The scary thing is the items labeled warning, I can barely see."

Can we awaken every day and talk ourselves into joyful acceptance of whatever we encounter? Can we find something to laugh about daily? Is laughter better than medicine? Can our thoughts sometimes predict our health, whether good or bad?

Eleanor Williams-Curry
4/08/05

TWELVE ACTS OF RACIAL HARMONIOUS LIVING

1. Become aware of other people's attitudes, ideas and culture. Start today to find a new way.

2. Before crossing the bridge, remove the barriers of anger and guilt. Start today to rid the things that divide.

3. Search for content of character, not the color of skin. This will become an awesome Journey.

4. Check out the daily dozen duties and eliminate division from the list. Suddenly the priorities change.

5. Redefine freedom for all and help it happen. Let freedom rise from within. It certainly won't trickle down.

6. Open up your heart. Practice being kind one to another. Whatever happened to good manners. Just say "Good morning."

7. Find out what tickles the person, makes them tick and what ticks them off. Now this works! This is called 'close proximity.'

8. Practice love that covers a multitude of sin. Love is the most underused action, yet the most powerful in the world.

9. Find a new reality that will transcend class, race and division. Start today. Have you already started?

10. No more whipping posts. Let go of any past grievances by being friendly. Start today. Who knows what tomorrow will say?

11. Prejudice is taught. Respond to the issue and how to resolve it. Keep your mind and heart ready for bouts of prejudice and create a knockout.

12. Unite fellowship and enjoy the differences. Find what we have in common. Start today.

Eleanor Williams-Curry

2/27/03

26 Days to Change our Children:

1. Attitude changing. "Good morning." "Have a good day". "Good night".
2. Boundaries help keep the internal strength while dealing with external pressures.
3. Character building means being connected and accepting change.
4. Desires and instant gratification can be risky. Know that discrimination is still alive and damaging.
5. Enthusiastic education energizes everyone.
6. Faith unseen beats fear. However, "behave right now, because our family does not act like that".
7. Gentleness brings comfort to others.
8. Heartfelt thinking, honesty and daily hugs motivate both giver and receiver.
9. Inclusive integration was decreed by law in 1954. "Freedom now! Yes!"
10. Joy removes burdens, making room for real happiness and peace.
11. Display kindness and seek knowledge.
12. Love yourself and others. "Jesus loves me, this I know". A lie poisons our lives.
13. Male voices. Money saved. Know that Media images are slanted.
14. Narrow paths are the best. Saying "No" to another, sometimes means to grow.
15. Opinions. Are your children obese? In others words 'too fat?' Can you change that?
16. Parental praise, purpose and perseverance are enhancers. A prejudicial act makes people seem crazy.
17. Attentive questions from children increase learning.
18. Read out loud with children, by taking turns. Respect what's right.
19. Recognize school is the student's Job. Smiling and singing wrecks depression. "Seeking something for nothing never happens".
20. Think that teachers are taking your place. Meet the teacher. Technology & Science are here for all children.
21. Unities in our families, with our children and on the job, build relationships.
22. Victory is the outgrowth of vision planning.
23. Do not whip children. Teach them non-violence. Good things come to those who work.
24. No more excuses. "Addictions can shorten one's life".
25. You are making a positive difference. "Acknowledge somebody today".
26. Know the zones of war, in the schools, from drugs, in the streets and the prisons. Protect the children.

I, the undersigned, shall instill these lessons to encourage children to grow up to be the best American citizens possible.

_____Date_____

The Endurance Wisdom Chest. By Eleanor Williams-Curry 1/01/2008

FIVE STAGES OF CHILD DEVELOPMENT

"Train up a child in the way he should go, and when he is old, he will not depart from it." (Prov.22-6)

First Five Years

Birth to 1 Year. TRUST. Babies are hungry, need diapers changed. Mistrust results from not being taken care of adequately. A sense of trust is vital to a baby's early development.

"I'm going to be taken care of, no matter what happens", becomes an internal reality. Anticipating their needs and doing what is necessary before the baby becomes agitated is a good habit.

2 Years to 4 Years. AUTONOMY. Walking and talking. Make your house childproof. Move book cases out of the way and put vases away. Let them go and enjoy the house. Yet stay ever alert to their movements. The famous challenge of saying "No" enters the 2 years old as the best expression. The major socialization in our house was attending Church. This happens once a baby was born. Going to Church is not a choice. It is a duty understood.

External Journeys

5 Years to 8 Years. INITATIVE. School and community activities start interaction with others. Playtime is important. Some organizational structure might be good, yet should not over extend the child's time. Initiate relationships to learn the true meaning of sharing and learning.

9 Years to 12 Years. INDUSTRY. Development of work ethic starts at home. Learn to assign simple chores. Teach 'whatever one starts, then finish it'. Teach how 'doing it right the first time saves time'. Adults mess up 'doing it for them'. Spanking, scolding and chastising creates disappointment. This discourages kids from being industrious. Frequent criticism is worse than slapping the child. Never use words such as stupid and dumb to describe any child. Eliminate constant frowns of disapproval.

Incredible Teens

13 Years to 18 Years. SELF IDENTITY. Most important stage of life for teens. "Who we are, separate from our parents?" It seems the easiest way to do the opposite of what parents says, suddenly matters. This is a time to figure out where they are in life. We've got to let them experience some things for themselves. One has to hold the reigns, but not too tight, and not too easy. A mistake often prepares the student for greater lessons. A mistake is a temporary failure, but not final. It is not how you start out. It's where you end up.

Sources: Alfred Gales, Administrative Trainer, San Jose, California

Endurance Wisdom Chest by Eleanor Williams – Curry, San Carlos, California

5/10/08

THE POWER of COMPASSION

C   Courage is withstanding the test for someone who is defenseless.

     Be of good cheer.

O   Offer raising the praise without any endings called "But!"

M   Mind and heart must be balanced. Every person thinks they are right.

     But God ponders the heart.

P   Possible are all things for them who believe. Hearts might be comforted,

     being knit together in love,

     And all the riches of full assurance of understanding,

     to the acknowledgement of the mystery of God.

A   Admonish one another with care.

     Yet assume another person is not above us or beneath us.

S   Serve one another. Love your neighbor as you love yourself. Love is active.

S   Stress can be eliminated. Start to smile. Sing a song. Shout a joyful noise.

I   Important people are the others, who strengthen us from their neediness.

O   Open the door, since opportunities are open for those who are ready.

N   Now is the time to seek the good things in life for yourself and others.

From the Endurance Wisdom Chest

Of Eleanor Williams-Curry

9/06/08

For extraordinary and constructive leadership by helping all students (K-12) in the district plus, authentic assistance to the administrators and her high regard for the professional teachers.

-San Mateo Elementary Teachers Association Award

A Lifetime Achievement Award for many years of service to the African-American Community and the Bay Area Committees at large. The 1996 Olympic Torch is bestowed to Eleanor Curry for advocating self –control in the minds of youth encouraging positive character building.

-United Way of the Bay Area, San Francisco, California

1980 ABE LINCOLN NATIONAL MERIT AWARD for exceptional Achievement as a Broadcaster and Citizen.

-Southern Baptist Radio and Television Commission

San Mateo County Women's Hall of Fame in recognition of Eleanor Curry for extraordinary achievements and contributions, 1994

-County of San Mateo, Redwood City, California

Appreciation for the establishment of the Curry Award for Girls and Young Women. The young women may have undergone hardships related to possible ethnic or racial discrimination, physical disability or the choice of nontraditional areas of study.

-Peninsular Community Foundation, San Mateo County

Eleanor Curry has shown exceptional dedication and responsiveness to the community. She has created opportunities for people where none existed. She has fostered communication among people with different points of view, and she has helped them to reach collaborative solutions. Eleanor's generous humanitarian spirit has been an inspiration to others and a catalyst for positive change in San Mateo County.

-The 1987 San Francisco Foundation Award

Epilog:

Solid racial relationships can work in the United States of America. We are ALL Americans. Now is the time to come together. If not now, when?

About the Author

Eleanor Curry is a Community Organizer, wife, mother, grandmother, and great grandmother plus, an advocate for children and their families. Eleanor's major accomplishment was creating the Curry Scholarship Award for low income teen girls on the Peninsula. She attended Antioch College/West receiving her B.A. Degree in Human Relations and Creative Arts. Eleanor lives with her husband in San Carlos, California.